12/12

JUMP!

JUMPING SPIDERS

Lynette Robbins

PowerKiDS
press™

New York

To Amber

Published in 2012 by The Rosen Publishing Group, Inc.
29 East 21st Street, New York, NY 10010

First Edition

Editor: Joanne Randolph
Book Design: Ashley Drago and Erica Clendening

Photo Credits: Cover, pp. 6, 8, 9 (right) 10, 12–13, 14, 17 (left), 18, 20 Shutterstock.com; p. 4 Oxford Scientific/Getty Images; pp. 5, 15, 16 © www.iStockphoto.com/Cathy Keifer; p. 7 © FLPA/Fabio Pupin/age fotostock; p. 9 (left) iStockphoto/Thinkstock; p. 11 © Rauschen Stream/age fotostock; p. 17 (right) George Grall/Getty Images; p. 19 © www.iStockphoto.com/James Benet; p. 21 © Hecker/Sauer/age fotostock; p. 22 © www.iStockphoto.com/Stéphane Bidouze.

Library of Congress Cataloging-in-Publication Data

Robbins, Lynette.
  Jumping spiders / by Lynette Robbins. — 1st ed.
     p. cm. — (Jump!)
  Includes index.
  ISBN 978-1-4488-5016-7 (library binding) — ISBN 978-1-4488-5165-2 (pbk.) — ISBN 978-1-4488-5166-9 (6-pack)
  1. Jumping spiders—Juvenile literature. I. Title.
  QL458.42.S24R63 2012
  595.4'4—dc22

                                    2011004167

Manufactured in the United States of America

CPSIA Compliance Information: Batch #WS11PK: For Further Information contact Rosen Publishing, New York, New York at 1-800-237-9932

Contents

Jump This Way, Jumping Spider!

Have you ever seen a jumping spider? Maybe you have seen one hopping along outside or in your house.

If you get close to a jumping spider, it may look back at you with its large eyes. It may even try to jump on you. Do not worry if it does. Most jumping spiders do

Jumping spiders get their name because they often jump from place to place. Jumping spiders can jump many times farther than their own body length.

not bite people. If a jumping spider jumps on you, be sure to handle it carefully so that you do not hurt it.

Jumping spiders are **arachnids**. All arachnids have eight legs. Scorpions, mites, and ticks are also arachnids.

This jumping spider is waiting for a bug to pass by. If a bug comes close, the jumping spider will jump on it, bite it, and enjoy some lunch!

No Web

Jumping spiders can be found all over the world. Many kinds of jumping spiders live in tropical rain forests. They can also be found in **temperate** forests, scrublands, deserts, and even mountains.

Unlike other kinds of spiders, jumping spiders do not make webs for catching food. Instead, they use their **silk** to make nests. Most jumping spiders

Some jumping spiders, such as this one resting on some pinecones, make their homes in forests.

make their nests in small spaces. A jumping spider may make its nest under a piece of bark or in a crack between rocks. Many jumping spiders make their nests between two leaves. Jumping spiders sleep in their nests at night.

This jumping spider is outside its nest hole in Italy.

So Many Spiders

There are more than 5,000 different kinds of jumping spiders! There are more kinds of jumping spiders than there are any other kind of spider. Jumping spiders are not very big. Most are about the size of the eraser on your pencil. Even the largest jumping spiders are less than 1 inch (2.5 cm) long.

Like all spiders, jumping spiders have two main body parts. The front body part is called the **cephalothorax.**

Jumping spiders can be brightly colored, as this one is. Males are often more colorful than females of the same kind.

The spider's head is part of the cephalothorax. The back body part is called the **abdomen**.

Some jumping spiders have hair on their bodies. Many jumping spiders are brightly colored. Most jumping spiders have rectangular faces.

ABOVE: All spiders have eight legs. They also have two short leglike parts near their mouths, called pedipalps or palps. You can clearly see the palps on this jumping spider.

RIGHT: Here you can see the two main body parts of this yellow jumping spider. The spider's legs are attached to its cephalothorax.

9

Jump, Spider, Jump!

Some kinds of jumping spiders can jump up to 40 times their own length. If you could jump like these jumping spiders, you would be able to jump over four school buses!

Jumping spiders do not have big **muscles** like other jumping animals. Most of the time, a jumping spider's legs are bent. When a jumping spider is ready to jump, it **expands** certain

Jumping spiders jump by quickly straightening their bent legs.

muscles in its body. This causes its back legs to fill quickly with liquid from inside its body. The liquid causes the spider's legs to straighten, which sends it bounding into the air. Jumping spiders can almost always land exactly where they want to when they jump.

Just as other spiders can, jumping spiders can make silk threads. A jumping spider spins a thread called a dragline before it jumps. It fixes the dragline to whatever it is sitting on.

Jumping Spider Facts

A jumping spider will use its silk to make a safety line before it jumps. If it misses the spot where it wants to land, it can climb back up the silk and try again.

1

5

When many animals look at television screens, they see only jumbles of moving dots. Jumping spiders, though, may be able to see the images. Researchers have seen jumping spiders react to flies and spiders on TV.

2

Jumping spiders have been found on Mount Everest, the tallest mountain in the world!

3

Males and females often look very different, even when they are the same kind of jumping spider. The male may be skinnier and have brighter colors.

4

A jumping spider's eyes take up almost as much space as its brain.

6

Jumping spiders use **poison** to stop their **prey** from moving. The poison comes from the spider's fangs.

7

There are more than 300 different kinds of jumping spiders in North America.

8

Jumping spiders have two claws on the ends of each leg. They use their claws to grab on to whatever they are landing on.

9

Most jumping spiders live for only a few months. Some live up to two years, though.

The Eyes Have It

Did you know that a jumping spider has eight eyes? Its two biggest eyes are on its face. They face straight ahead. There is a smaller eye to the side of each of the big eyes. The other four eyes are small. They can be on the sides and back or on the top of the spider's cephalothorax.

Jumping spiders are known for their large eyes. They need great vision because they go out and hunt for food instead of waiting for it to get caught in a web.

Unlike most spiders, jumping spiders' large eyes see very well. They can see colors, objects, and movement. The smaller eyes can sense only movement. Because a jumping spider has eyes all around its cephalothorax, it can sense movement from any direction.

Jumping spiders hunt by watching and waiting. They follow the movement of nearby insects, move themselves closer, and wait for the right moment to jump on them.

Jumping on Dinner

Jumping spiders are meat eaters. They eat all kinds of insects and other spiders. Jumping spiders use their sharp eyesight and jumping skills to hunt.

A jumping spider sneaks up on its prey. Slowly, it creeps closer and closer. Then, suddenly, it jumps! It lands on top of the unlucky insect and digs its fangs into the insect's body.

This spider has caught a fly. When it catches a bug, it puts poison into its body with its fangs.

A jumping spider must be careful when it is attacking a large insect or spider. It could easily be eaten by its prey, instead of the other way around. Large insects, other spiders, birds, and lizards all eat jumping spiders.

ABOVE: As do all spiders, jumping spiders put a special fluid into their prey that turns its insides into a watery matter that they can then drink.

RIGHT: This jumping spider has caught and is eating a caterpillar.

17

Fighting and Adapting

Jumping spiders spend nearly all their lives alone. If two male jumping spiders meet, they are likely to fight. The loser may be killed, or it may run away when it realizes it has been beaten.

Some kinds of jumping spiders have **adapted** over time to look more like ants than spiders.

This kind of jumping spider has adapted over time to look like an ant. Its legs are thinner than those of other kinds of spiders. It has mouthparts that look more like an ant's, too.

These spiders look like they have the three body parts of insects. They also walk like ants and wave their front legs around in the air, the way ants do with their **antennae**. Looking like ants keeps these spiders safe from **predators**. Ants bite hard and taste bad. Many predators do not eat them.

This is another jumping spider that looks like an ant. Some spiders that look like ants have adapted to walking around in groups, as ants do. Most spiders live alone.

Making More Spiders

The only time jumping spiders look for company is when they want to **mate**. In order to mate with a female, a male jumping spider must dance for her. The male spider bobs, zigzags, and waves his legs and **palps** in the air for her. He shows her the bright colors on his body. The female may decide to mate with him, or she may just eat him instead.

Female jumping spiders may make their nests under leaves, as this one has done.

Once a female has mated, she lays her eggs in her nest. She keeps them safe by using her silk to make an egg sac. When the eggs hatch, the baby spiders look like tiny adult spiders. Female jumping spiders often guard their eggs and stay with their babies until they leave the nest.

This jumping spider mother is guarding her babies until they can leave the nest.

Our Friend the Jumping Spider

Jumping spiders are an important part of the **food chain**. They are food for bigger animals, such as snakes, lizards, birds, and rodents. In turn, when jumping spiders eat insects, they help keep their ecosystem in balance.

You might think jumping spiders look scary or cute. Either way, these spiders are interesting and important arachnids!

Many people like jumping spiders because they eat insects that are thought to be pests. When jumping spiders eat grasshoppers, they help keep them out of our gardens. When jumping spiders eat mosquitoes and flies, they keep those insects from biting us. Next time you see a jumping spider, remember that it is your friend!

Glossary

abdomen (AB-duh-mun) The large, back part of an insect's or arachnid's body.

adapted (uh-DAPT-ed) Changed to fit new conditions.

antennae (an-TEH-nee) Thin, rodlike feelers on the heads of certain animals.

arachnids (uh-RAK-nidz) A type of animal that includes spiders and ticks.

cephalothorax (se-fuh-luh-THOR-aks) A spider's front body part, containing its head and chest.

expands (ek-SPANDZ) Spreads out, or grows larger.

food chain (FOOD CHAYN) A group of living things that are each other's food.

mate (MAYT) To come together to make babies.

muscles (MUH-sulz) Parts of the body that make the body move.

palps (PALPS) Small, fingerlike parts of an insect's or arachnid's mouth.

poison (POY-zun) Matter that can cause pain or death.

predators (PREH-duh-terz) Animals that kill other animals for food.

prey (PRAY) An animal that is hunted by another animal for food.

silk (SILK) Something made by a spider's body that the spider uses to make webs, things to help it catch food, or nests.

temperate (TEM-puh-rut) Not too hot or too cold.

Index

A
arachnids, 5

E
eye(s), 4, 13–15

F
food chain, 22

forests, 6

M
mites, 5

mountain(s), 6, 13

muscles, 10–11

P
palps, 20

poison, 13

predators, 19

R
rodents, 22

S
scorpions, 5

silk, 6, 12, 21

W
webs, 6

Web Sites

Due to the changing nature of Internet links, PowerKids Press has developed an online list of Web sites related to the subject of this book. This site is updated regularly. Please use this link to access the list:
www.powerkidslinks.com/jump/spiders/